# J...
## of Scripture to
# Handle Today

Secrets for navigating
your life
with ease and peace

# MARILYN LOVE

Published by
Impact Driven Publishing
3129 S. Hacienda Boulevard, Suite #658
Hacienda Heights, CA 91745

Manufactured in the United States of America, or in the United Kingdom when distributed elsewhere.

Love, Marilyn.
*JUST A PINCH of Scripture to Handle TODAY*
    ISBN: 978-1-7347528-7-8
    eBook: 978-1-7347528-8-5
    LCCN: 2023905358

Cover design by: Julia Kuris
Copyediting by: Wendie Pecharsky
Interior design by: Suba Murugan
Author photo by: Larry Crandall Photography
Brand Graphics Development by: Cristian Magdil and Launch Spectrum

https://JustSayTheWord.Love

What People Are Saying About The
Importance of this book:

# Just A Pinch
## of Scripture to
# Handle Today
### Secrets for navigating your life
### with ease and peace

and of the Brand:

## *JUST SAY THE WORD!*
### Reclaiming YOU. Reconnecting to GOD.

"Marilyn, I appreciate your weekly Pinch messages. Your analogies are spot on. Now I'm able to have clarity about lessons from Sunday School that I didn't understand. I'm not well versed in the Bible, nor do I have any church ties; but I feel a keen connection to our Heavenly Father because of the way you deliver messages of belief, faith, commitment, and the power of prayer. Keep doing what you do."

**Carol D. Snuggs**
Experienced Contracts Manager

"Marilyn you have a gift to write, thanks for sharing this powerful message with us. May God continue to bless and use you graciously."

**Pastor Gail Caprietta**
Author, Minister, Aquatic Fitness Professional

"I shared your message with a friend who was having a difficult week. She said she felt like God sent it for her exactly when she needed it. She was very appreciative!"

**Harriet Brown**
Academic Advisor

## WHAT PEOPLE ARE SAYING

"Awesome word of testimony. Thank you for the reminder to put God first in all that we do. Blessings to you."

**Elaine Proctor**
Retired Clinical Analyzer

"Thank you, Marilyn, for profound words. Always on time and much needed now. Be blessed."

**Lydia Turner**
Retired Distributions Manager

"Thank you for your encouragement each week. God has given you a great gift."

**Diane Evans**
Retired Auto Industry Janitor

"Thanks so much, Marilyn. I am so grateful for your Wednesday texts that help carry me through the week."

**Harriet Brown**
Academic Advisor

"I understood everything you said! I love the breakdown of scripture!! That was so awesome! Thank you for your obedience to God's vision! Every Wednesday I look forward to your God given word!"

**Beatriz Nieves**

CEO, RISE UP Long Beach Youth Non-Profit

"Amen. I think your message is a reminder that we didn't get here by ourselves, meaning our successes in life came from God either directly or indirectly. God finds mysterious ways to help us and to help us help others. Thank you Marilyn. You are amazing."

**Dr. Candace Davis**

Owner, ChiroMed Healing Center

"Every part was meaningful and on point!!! Especially walking in and stirring up our gifts of power, love, and a sound mind; such a powerful concept. As well as doing the right thing because it's the right thing to do before the Lord, by exemplifying God's divine truth daily. Again, another phenomenal lesson and for that I am truly blessed. Thank you!"

**Jan Cox**

Therapist, Clinical Supervisor

"Good morning Sistah Marilyn. I just read the Pinch message and it is full of confirmation for the Bible Studies that our ministry team has taught over the last few weeks. I want to share this AWESOME message with them!!! Thanks for the confirmation."

**Louise Atkins-Dodson**

Retired Deputy Probation Officer

"I'm always amazed at how the Holy Spirit uses you to provide just what I need to hear in that moment. Thank you for your obedience in sharing what has been put on your heart. Love you!"

**Patrice Rice**

High School Administrator

"Amen!! Preach Girl!! Thanks for the encouragement to step out on faith. We know what our God can do but we don't think we're worthy, and I'm speaking for me! Thanking God for His Holy Word through you."

**Wanda Gregory Mobley**

Business Owner

"Marilyn, continue to let the Lord use you and continue to share with us. We all benefit from your weekly devotion."

**Gwen Bayard-Hall**
Retired Assistant Director

"Thank you, Marilyn, for being so faithful and diligent in reaching out to us week after week. Be encouraged and continue to allow the Lord to use you, knowing what you give to us each week will not return void. There really is power in the name of Jesus. Love you girl."

**Joni Wright**

"God is faithful, Marilyn, and as you continue to bless us with your godly wisdom, expect His blessings to flow – exceedingly above all you can ask for in life. Bless you for taking time out to challenge us with taking a stand on the Word of God. You are a tremendous blessing to me and the Quilt Sisters. Much love."

**Regina Covington-Todd**
Retired Educator

# WHAT PEOPLE ARE SAYING

"I thought this was from your pastor. Don't stop! I look forward to your weekly message!"

**Edward Douglas Moody**
Retired Military

"Amen! Thank you, my sister, for your diligence and faithfulness as you bless me every week with these momentums of truth."

**LeJon Stanley**
Retired Transportation Operator

"Girl!!! Thank you so very much for sharing this word today. I really need it right now."

**Michelle Love**
Executive Administrative Assistant

"My Sister, thank you for today's inspirational message. It was right on time! Just like God!"

**Joy Rice**
Human Resources Technician

"Thank you, Cousin Marilyn. Very encouraging and uplifting."

**Linda Moody**
Retired Customer Service Representative

"Thank you, Marilyn, for today's word. I really needed it."

**Gloria Albert Matthews**
Special Education Assistant

"Great word as always Marilyn; right on time. I'm currently struggling with fear and doubt about a couple of things in my life. And I'm so tempted to make abrupt decisions just to get resolution. But, knowing that things will work themselves out in God's time and not my own is keeping me from rushing things. Today's Pinch is confirmation that I get to trust the Lord. Thank you so much."

**Carol D. Snuggs**
Experienced Contracts Manager

# WHAT PEOPLE ARE SAYING

"One of the highlights of my week is waiting with tip-toe anticipation to receive Marilyn's weekly Pinch messages on Wednesdays. The messages always come just at the right time and always provide me just the encouragement I need to continue in my Christian walk for the week. I am so glad to see Marilyn is turning the weekly 'pinches' into a book – that way I can go back and read them at my leisure and as a constant reminder of God's word and His unfailing love for us, His children. Thank you, Marilyn, for your commitment and dedication to this work. God is doing a great thing through you!"

**Angela Reddock-Wright, Esq.**
Employment Mediator

"I am honored and grateful that God put this amazing human being, Marilyn Love, in my life more than 40 years ago. We've grown together in Christ and throughout the years I've watched her go through heartbreak, mistakes, unbearable pain, and life's circumstances in general, coming out with both her hands up yet choosing to praise God. When she rededicated her life to God, a miraculous transformation occurred in her that also affected me. As her love for God grew, so did her commitment to bring comfort, hope, love, and peace to all whose paths she crossed. She is the embodiment of courage, resilience, wisdom and is unique, grounded, compassionate, and has no problem taking that first step into unfamiliar territory.

Her encouragement, understanding, and ability to express the word of God in stories and quotes is phenomenal. Her Pinch ministry is a great accomplishment and a gift one can return to again and again for reference and refreshing. The devotionals remind us about how great our God is and how great He is in us! She plays an essential role in God's loving plan of salvation. Even now, while teaching English as a Second Language, she is an example of God's love to a diverse collection of cultures. I know that this book, the devotionals, and future endeavors will equip, strengthen, and bless all who partake. I'm so blessed and happy that she's my friend, confidante, and Sister-in-Christ for life."

**Rhea Rouse**

Benefits Administrator, and a long-time friend

# Acknowledgements

First, I give all thanks, honor, and glory to God for placing His purpose inside me, and for choosing me to write this book. To my Quilt Sisters, the first recipients of what evolved into weekly Just a Pinch text messages, thank you for being the fertile ground where this journey began. To all recipients of my weekly Just a Pinch text messages, which includes longtime friends, newly acquired friends, family members, fellow church members, a Christian bookstore owner, and former co-workers, I am grateful for your prayers, encouragement, and confirmation that the messages you received were just what you needed—when you needed it. Many of you also encouraged me to write a book – which I appreciate. I consider you as vital contributors to this journey. I give special thanks to my friend, chiropractor, and fellow Quilt Sister Dr. Candace Davis, who said "you should write a book, and I know a man who can help you." Special thanks go to that man - Rich Kozak, Founder of RichBrands and IMPACT DRIVEN Publishing - for guiding me through the Brand Development process and shining a mirror upon me so I could see what's inside me. Through Rich's guidance and expertise in Brand Development, this "book" has become a stake in the ground to move my brand, *JUST SAY THE WORD!*, forward. This book is the first in a series of seven books that you will see on the shelves in the very near future.

I have had the privilege to worship in different denominations – all of which taught the love of God and His son Jesus. I am grateful to each one for feeding into my soul. I give thanks to the church of my early years, Grant African Methodist Episcopal Church, Long Beach, CA, for being instrumental in my upbringing as the place where my foundation was formed. To the place I call my second church, Carson Community Deliverance Center (CCDC), Carson, CA, I give thanks for being the place where I received numerous spiritual breakthroughs while visiting for special events and

# ACKNOWLEDGEMENTS

Monday Night Prayer. I give heartfelt thanks and gratitude to the members of CCDC (especially my bff Rhea Rouse who initially invited me), and the late Bishop Grate and late First Lady Patty Shipp for their love, spiritual worship, support, and words of affirmation that I still refer to. To my current church, Zoe Center (formerly Zoe Christian Fellowship of Whittier, CA), I give thanks for being the place where I met and received The Holy Spirit, and where my spiritual growth continues. Bishop Ed and First Lady Vanessa Smith, your love for God, your transparency in all areas of your lives, and the ways you have shepherded me over the years as a member of Zoe have been a driving force in me discovering that I have a purpose. I love you, I thank God for you, and I thank you.

My mother and father were my greatest inspiration, having lived through Jim Crow in the south and still serving this country and our community with honor. I am today's Marilyn because of their examples of love, strength, integrity, and determination. I thank my parents, Ocie and Clara Love, for giving me life and for loving me even when I made them shake their heads in utter disbelief because of something I did.

I am thankful for the family God blessed me with. My siblings Linda, Connie (and long-time companion Herbert), and Michael (and his wife Michelle), my daughter Rachel, my nephew Steven (and his wife Anna), my niece Stacey, and numerous cousins whom I love deeply. God is truly a God of miracles. In 2012 when I discovered that we have an older sister, Lois (and her husband Robert), and a niece Kim, my heart was expanded in a wonderful way. I cannot imagine my life without them! I am grateful for the opportunity God gave me to be a bonus mom to Deborah, Shantelle, and Starr. I cherish our relationship. God has also blessed me with many friends who have become my non-biological family. If I named them all, I would fill [nearly] every page of this book. I cherish my Love, Moody, Harmon, Emerson and Moss DNA. There is greatness in those roots. I'm also thankful for my honorary non-DNA families: Meyers, Covington, Rice, Leaming, Bird, Vines, Gerken, and Nieves. God brought you all into my life at just the right time, just the right season. I love you all!

# ACKNOWLEDGEMENTS

Myrtle Avenue, the street where I grew up, gave me so many wonderful experiences and memories. I am deeply appreciative to the families who all had a hand in raising me: Shepherd, Henderson, Johnson, Sublette, Morton, West, Fountain, Hill, Strong, Hopson, King, and Booth. The African adage says: "It takes a village to raise a child." You were my village, and I will always carry your words of encouragement, scolding, and life lessons within my heart.

Beauty for ashes describes the circumstances upon which my purpose began. If you met Tammie, you would never know how much she has overcome. Her strength and ability to always love earned her the endearment name "Sista Luv." This book would not exist had she not survived the tragic event of March 8, 2008. Thank you for being my sister from another mom and mister. I love you effortlessly and endlessly.

God has been my source and the rock upon which I could always lean in good times and when going through trials. He never let me fall. He was never out of reach. Even when I did not look to God first, He was always right there when I came to my senses and remembered what a friend I have in Him. That same friend is available and waiting for you.

Welcome to the beginning of something big, delivered in Just A Pinch.

# Table of Contents

What People Are Saying About the Importance of this Book

# CHAPTER 1

# THE POWER OF A PINCH:
## *A Little Goes A Long Way*

**S**ometimes a little thing, like a pinch, is perfect. Not too much, not too little. Just right!

The concept of a pinch has so many variations. Perhaps you're familiar with the sayings "a little goes a long way," or "don't overdo it." A pinch can indicate that at this moment, a small amount of something can be just enough and all you need.

Think of information given a pinch at a time as similar to eating a delicious meal a bite at a time. Savoring each bite allows one to experience tastes, textures, aromas, and flavors. All of the goodness available in each bite makes one look forward to the next bite. A pinch of information that touches one's needs, emotions, and senses can pique curiosity about what the next pinch will reveal. And we know that food and information are both easier to digest a pinch at a time. Think about the opposite: a large data dump of information brings the same effect as having a mouth stuffed full of food to the point that chewing becomes difficult. Tasting and enjoying each flavor or each nuance of information is not possible, and digesting it all is challenging.

It feels good when you're not overwhelmed with information. That good feeling can spark your desire to continue where you left off. It might even give you the drive and desire to look forward to more. And it feels good when your curiosity gets "a pinch."

**How to trust that a pinch so small can do so much.**

In the kitchen, a pinch of salt is a critical ingredient in preparing your food. Imagine a pot of soup—fresh

## THE POWER OF A PINCH:

chicken noodle, minestrone, beef barley, tomato bisque, and clam chowder. A pinch of salt enhances the flavors of the ingredients of the soup. Your favorite baked goods rely on a pinch of salt—salt controls yeast growth when baking bread. In cakes and cookies, the ions in salt eliminate bitterness.

When does a pinch of salt become a critical ingredient in handling your life today—something small that brings enhancement to the flavors of the elements of your life and eliminates bitterness? What if that pinch were found within the pages of a book? This book was written to serve you the pinch that your spirit, soul, and life need. Do you have it in you to trust that a pinch so small can do so much? Yes? Read on!

# CHAPTER 2

# KNOW IT'S NO ACCIDENT:

*To Know Now What You Didn't*

*Know Then*

**S**uch a loud whisper. Did anyone else hear it? What if it's only meant for me?

You heard it—the whisper. Even though it was a whisper, you heard it loud and clear. It told you to do it, or it told you to *not* do it. You listened and followed through. Because of the whisper, you avoided something harmful: an accident, choosing the wrong job, or the wrong mate. Because of the whisper, you received something beneficial: a promotion on the job, green lights all the way to your destination, and a pair of shoes that were still comfortable at the end of a long day.

You found out that the whisper was correct. You thought for a moment, and then you said it...

You said—*something* told me. The thing you did when you heard the whisper was not what you planned to do. You planned to do the exact opposite, but *something* steered you in the right direction. It turns out that *something* has your best interests at heart.

Now that *something* has your attention, you begin to notice a feeling...

You felt it—a tugging sensation inside of you, and it has your attention. It is urging you to step out, to be courageous enough to take the action that you've been avoiding. It is telling you that this is your time, that you are capable, and you have what it takes.

But then you follow these revelations with thoughts of not feeling worthy, thinking these things don't happen to you. In the midst awaits negativity (fear), hiding in the bushes waiting for you to step out so it can pounce on you. With it comes doubt, trying to unpack its suitcase of phrases that begin with "you can't, you won't, you don't know how to, you don't have what it takes, no one in your family has ever," and a plethora of other lies and put-downs. Now you're believing that these things don't happen to you, so why bother? All the while, in this critical time, *something* continues to whisper to you, with messages that are meant for your ears, whispers that bring you to the other side of fear, the other side of doubt, the other side of negativity. If the noise of fear is allowed to become increasingly louder, you might not hear the reassuring whispers of *something*.

Now you ask yourself, "Do these things happen to people like me?" Well, they do. What you're going through is not an accident.

**Yeah, but this kind of stuff never happens to me!**
If you're a person who thinks you're *not as worthy* as other people because of _____ (you fill in the blank), then I want you to kindly ask yourself this question:

## KNOW IT'S NO ACCIDENT:

How is that *not-as-worthy* thinking working out for you? Is it keeping you from taking action? Does it allow fear to get between you and achieving your goals? Does it hold you back? Has it limited the possibilities that existed or that you see for your life? Do you defer opportunities to others? Do you not step into the reason you're here? Does it keep you from touching others' lives and helping them grow and heal? When you have those *not-as-worthy* thoughts, how do those thoughts work out for you?

**Just face it, you deserve all of this and more.**
Don't be surprised if, as you were reading, you noticed instances when your head nodded in agreement. Perhaps something struck a chord of familiarity with you. You might have felt a warm reassurance about yourself and what you are capable of. But then you might have seen your warm flames of reassurance doused by a chilling stream of fear, doubt, or disbelief.

The great thing about warm flames of reassurance is they are often resilient—not extinguishable by a little stream of fear or doubt or disbelief. There is often a glowing ember that will be reignited by the confidence you gain when you allow yourself to hear those whispers of *something*.

## The right place, the right time.

Life gives opportunities to us that feel like the right place and the right time. Have you ever felt it was the right place, the right time, and you *missed* your opportunity? So far in this book, what you have read about hearing, about seeing, and about feeling is an invitation for you to consider that this book and what it shares are the right place and the right time for *you*.

# CHAPTER 3

# WHEN GOD SENDS YOU A TEXT, WILL YOU READ IT?

*How Will You Know It's Your Time?*

G od's "caller ID" is within your own spirit.

Are you struggling with the roadblock question "Why am I receiving these whispers from *something*— why me?" In case you are, let's take a moment to clear the road. Here is one answer: Why *not* you? Here is another answer: Because whether you know it or not, you are worthy. And since the third time is a charm, here is a third answer: Because *something* loves you. Let's reveal the identity of *"something."* If the possibility that *something* refers to God has crossed your mind, then you are correct. Think about those moments in your life when you heard the voice of *something,* and you received the correct answer and the perfect solution. Think about those moments when you saw things go well because you listened to and followed *something.* Think about those moments when you felt a gentle nudge from *something* that gave you the confidence to do or say what you thought you could not. In those moments, you experienced God.

---

**God has been speaking directly to your spirit, ever so gently.**

---

God has been speaking directly to your spirit, ever so gently. Those whispers were received because your spirit already has its own personal connection with God. Because of this connection, God's whispers are not rejected by an app that detects unwanted communication. They are not labeled as junk or sent to the spam folder. This connection happens because your spirit recognizes God's caller ID. This is why you can hear God's whispers. God and your spirit are patiently waiting for you to establish (or renew) a relationship with God. A personal connection that will enable you to recognize God's caller ID. God desires to tell you more, to show you more, and to allow you to feel His love more.

**Welcoming what's around you.**

Whether we choose to accept it or not, there are life lessons all around us. These lessons are filled with opportunities for change—some positive, some negative. When it comes to change, people often have two types of responses:

1. Welcoming change
2. Doing anything to avoid change

Which type are you? Do you welcome change, or do you avoid change? There is one thing both types have in common. They both benefit when led by loving guidance to show them *how* to welcome what is around them. In one way or another, change is an everyday occurrence happening all around us -- change is a part of life. Ironically, when we avoid the change around us, we change anyway, because now we have to adapt ourselves to living a life that decides to not embrace the change surrounding us.

**Blessings amid your journey.**
Your journey doesn't happen overnight. Just like the grains of salt in a pinch are small yet filled with flavor, your journey, taken a step at a time, is filled with blessings along the way. Allow yourself to embrace the blessings. You might find moments of blessings like these on your journey:

- The fresh scent in the air after the rain makes you aware of the fresh new beginnings in your life.
- You notice in a moment that what used to get under your skin doesn't bother you anymore.
- In a conversation, a person says something to you that gives you clarity.

- You stop during a walk and see beauty in a flower that gives you a feeling of peace and calm.
- You realize in a moment that the ingredients necessary for *your unique* journey have been inside you all along.
- You begin to experience an enhanced understanding of who you are.
- Your heart senses a closer relationship with God.

**Opening your heart in the right moment to what you do not see.**

Gaining the sense that God is the author of your life, you begin realizing that He knows what lies ahead long before you see it. When you open your heart to God, you make your heart available to allow His guidance and direction to lead you.

I want to take a moment and talk directly to you, about your right moment, right now. The marvels of technology have made it possible for me to do so. Throughout this book, whenever you see

### ❤ Love Speaks ❤

it means I have something to say directly to you in a short video message.

**Simply scan the QR Code with your phone or type the URL address into a browser and the video will appear.**

### ❤ Love Speaks ❤
*About Trusting God—A Winning Choice*

[https://JustSayTheWord.Love/WinningChoice](https://JustSayTheWord.Love/WinningChoice)

## What Happens if You Don't Open Your Heart?

What happens if you don't water a plant? The leaves will begin to droop and eventually it will wither away at the roots and die. What if you don't maintain your car? Over time, you will experience performance problems and quite possibly become stranded. Sometimes we're stranded in the wrong place.

Chapter 4 of the 23$^{rd}$ Psalm says, *"Even though **I walk through** the valley of the shadow of death, I will fear no evil, for you are with me; your rod and your staff they comfort me."*

Imagine being stranded in a real-life valley of the shadow of death situation, and you have not opened your heart. You are alone. Evil is all around you and you are filled with fear. You have no form of comfort.

Refusing to open your heart can have many "looks":

- It can look like someone who will not give God access to their heart.
- It can look like someone who refuses to listen to sound and helpful advice.
- It can look like someone who insists on doing things their way.

15

- It can look like someone who thinks they can handle any problem, challenge, or even danger.
- If you're not careful, it can look like you.

Many people wait until there is a big problem or danger in their life to then acknowledge their need for God. A funny-not-so-funny joke says that the loudest calls for God and Jesus come from an airplane full of non-believers spiraling downward and about to crash. My friend, your life does not have to take this path. God is always there, and you feel His love when you open your heart.

**You can ask God what He wants for you.**
People ask each other for advice. Sometimes they don't listen to the answer or even stick around to hear the answer. Perhaps you've experienced someone asking you for advice. You spend your time and maybe even resources to lovingly and caringly make sure you give them sound advice. And what do they do? They reject your advice or don't even listen.

God experiences this same behavior from us. His Word in the scriptures is wisdom-filled advice and direction to make our lives better, daily. Sadly, some people make a habit of not listening, essentially *refusing* to accept His Word. In contrast, while we might decide enough is enough and *avoid* the advice-seeking person, God stays right with us. He does not avoid us. He never gives up on us. He is lovingly and caringly always available, with a characteristic that we often run low on and admire in others—that characteristic is *loving patience*.

Sometimes it takes becoming *"sick and tired of being sick and tired"* for people to stop and listen, and learn about the "more" that life has in store for them. Truly, we don't always know. And even if we think we know, the best way to find out is to ask. God knows our life's path, and He has a purpose that is just for you.

## ❤ Love Speaks ❤
### *About God's Plan For You*

https://JustSayTheWord.Love/GodsPlanForYou

**Taking the limits off your trust.**

Sometimes, our thoughts, ideas, and feelings put limits on our ability to trust. Those limits deceive us and make us doubt ourselves, saying, "You can't," or, "You're not good enough," or, "You're not smart enough," or, "You don't know enough," or, "You're going to fail," or "People will talk about you," or other self-doubting, fearful mind tricks.

# WHEN GOD SENDS YOU A TEXT, WILL YOU READ IT?

When we put fear aside, allowing ourselves to trust, those limits fall away. By taking the limits off our trust, our innate power returns, unlimited. With the limits removed, you are ready to:

- Gratefully experience the unlimited ability to hear and follow God's Word.
- Powerfully reap the benefits of achieving goals.
- Positively enjoy upward movement in your life.

**For your eyes only: God has a timely message appropriate to your life right now.**
God's message "for your eyes only" is just for you, today, where you are in your life right now. God has known you since long before you were in your mother's womb. He knows the unlimited power He has given you. Sometimes, people think they must achieve some great accomplishment to receive what God has for them. This is not the case. There is no status required or title needed after your name. When you accept and receive God's message, God will position you in the place where He wants you.

**About Those Distractions Interrupting Your Focus.**

While doing something important, you check your cell phone. There was no immediate need for you to check your cell phone. It was a distraction. Some distractions require our immediate attention, such as a crying baby or a pot of soup boiling over; however, many distractions do not. Giving distractions our attention creates an interruption that guides us away from our focus in the short-run, and possibly away from our true purpose in the long run.

**God is ready for you**

God is ready for you to take control and step into your true purpose. Are *you*?

Are you allowing self-imposed limits to stop you?

Are you allowing distractions to guide you away from your focus on purpose?

If now is your time, if it's your time now, let the limits fall away.

He's waiting for you.

# WHEN GOD SENDS YOU A TEXT, WILL YOU READ IT?

### *Say The Word*—**Action Step 1:**

Imagine that, at three different times, God sends you the three TEXTs you will see on page 21.

Select one of these texts, consider how you would respond, authentically from your heart.
NOTE: We are providing empty space on the next page for you to write the response to God to the text message you select.

### Three (3) Text Messages from God to You:

**God's Text #1:** "My child, what is stopping you from trusting me?"

**God's Text #2:** "My strong and limitless child, how easy or difficult is it when you attempt to go at life on your own?"

**God's Text #3:** "My beloved child, you need to get something off your chest. What do you need to tell me?"

Select one (1) text message and write your response to God on the next page.

# CHAPTER 4

# SPEAKING OF SEASONING,
## *Making Sure You Arrive In The Right Season*

**T**hose seasons in your life.

Winter, spring, summer, fall—we know they're coming. Where you live in the world determines the type of temperature and landscape changes that accompany the changing seasons. We prepare for them in many ways, because being prepared is necessary. For example, winter clothes replace summer clothes in the closet. Hats, scarves, and gloves come out of storage bins. Pilot lights are lit on furnaces. Weatherstripping goes around doors and windows. Being season-ready is essential. There are also seasons in life. We need to prepare ourselves to be ready for the changes these seasons bring.

The Bible speaks about a variety of seasons in life in Chapter Three of the book of Ecclesiastes. Some of these seasons are a time:

> to plant and harvest,
> to cry and to laugh,
> to hold and to release,
> to keep silent and to speak,
> and many other seasons are named.

In life, when it comes to seasons and seasons coming, there is one thing that we all have in common, and that is this—we all go through them. We go through them, but we are not meant to stay there. There are lessons in the journeys through the seasons of life. During these journeys, we experience some bumps and bruises, successes, and failures along the way. As we survive the difficult ones, we emerge stronger and learn what to do and what to avoid doing. As we joyfully experience the positive ones, we gain a sense of growth and accomplishment, and perhaps even amazement as we learn to trust our inner spirit.

**You can weather the storms, whether it's a hurricane or a light rain shower.**

It is highly unlikely that anyone has a cape in their wardrobe that they can put on and be equipped with superhuman powers. Such power is something that none of us would be able to handle. However, there is a spiritual power source that knows what we need and when to give it to us, in exactly the right amount. On our own and with our limited knowledge, we can easily mistake a life situation of hurricane proportion for a light shower. Such an underestimation would make proper preparation next to impossible——on our own and with our limited knowledge. God is here with a sign directing us to His fortress of shelter where there is love and protection from the hurricanes of life. He is holding up an umbrella under which we will be warm and dry during the light showers that pass over us. Hurricanes and other challenges will come. When we allow the power of the spirit to guide us, we gain the wisdom to withstand whatever storm or challenge comes our way.

## ❤ Love Speaks ❤
### *About Answering the Question 'Why Me?'*

https://JustSayTheWord.Love/WhyMe

## Your season becomes right when you "arrive right."

What does it take to position yourself to "arrive right"? Let's begin by looking at the relationship we have with our mind, will, and spirit.

Our mind gives us options. When faced with a situation, it is our mind that decides how we react. Just like the seasons mentioned earlier, our mind chooses which season to operate in. To be positive or negative. To react maturely or childishly. To be selfless or selfish. To live in gratitude or criticism. To accept responsibility or to find fault. By listening to the voice within our spirit, we control the direction of the decisions our mind makes.

The responsibility of our will is to influence our minds to do the right thing. When your will is weak, you may experience results like being comfortable with your mind choosing to do something that you know you shouldn't have done. On the other hand, your will grows stronger when it wins a struggle like directing your mind to make a decision that positions you to be the bigger person versus egging on a negative situation. When we put God's will into our hearts, His will becomes our will. When His will becomes our will, we experience the spiritual growth necessary to strengthen our will to do the right things, the right way.

In life, we have warnings that protect us and keep us safe from potential danger. Yellow lights alert us to slow down and prepare to stop. A light on the surface of an electric cooktop stove lets us know it is still too hot to touch. Instructions on a child safety seat keep our little ones safe in the car. In our mind's eye, we can see what the consequences of ignoring these warnings might look like—the aftermath of a car accident, the blister from a burn on your finger, or a child's arm in a cast. Therefore, we observe these warnings, because avoiding them would result in serious injury or worse.

Some warnings alert you about potential dangers that affect your spirit. You have seen the warnings, and you understood them. Some spiritual warnings tell us to be humble, to offer a soft answer, to forgive, to show love, to treat others with kindness, to be gentle, and to be humble. They encourage us to control what we say, what we do, how we think, and how we react. Scriptures provide us with real examples of what these behaviors look like, by giving narratives of events in the lives of actual people. If you have stumbled or struggled with "getting it right" when it comes to spiritual warnings, ask yourself if it is because you ignored a spiritual warning for you to close the game app on your cell phone and open the Bible app to read just one scripture that is timely for you right now, today.

Spiritual warnings also have consequences that result from ignoring them. As with life warnings, you have also seen in your mind's eye the consequences of ignoring spiritual warnings. It was that image of being banned from your favorite restaurant after throwing a drink at the server for bringing you the wrong order. Or the image that showed you "slipping on a banana peel" in your life because you ignored someone at work you didn't care for who was trying to alert you to the danger. These would not have happened if you followed the warning to treat others with kindness. You have also heard the consequences. The sound of you stirring in bed unable to sleep, because the weight of unresolved issues that you've neglected for far too long is disturbing your peace. This would not happen if you followed the warning and read one scripture. You may have become comfortable ignoring these warnings because it seems like no harm was done. The consequence didn't happen, so in essence, you believe you got away with it. But, in reality, you didn't. Your spirit has needs. Your spirit needs you to protect it by providing a safe place for it to grow. One way to do this is by choosing to follow God's will. The other way is by acting upon that choice and taking the steps necessary to make changes. It's time for you to put an end to looking the other way. It's time for you to stop doing the very thing that the spiritual warnings are telling you to avoid. If you have become comfortable ignoring the warnings because it seemed like no harm was done, your spirit needs you to pay attention and observe the warnings with the same care and concern that you give to warnings that protect your life. Your spirit is crying out for you to take proper care of it. Your spirit is asking: What have you done for me lately?

**When you make time, it IS the right season.**
Making time and taking your time are opposites. Making time is an intentional act that is done to regularly work on a task. Taking your time looks more like: if I feel like working on a task, I might

do it, as long as there is not something else happening that I would rather do. People make time for what is important to them. What do you make time for? Make 10 minutes right now to write down five things (aside from family responsibilities, work, or school) that you make time for, from the most important to least important.

Now that you've made your list, is there anything nonessential? In other words, is there anything that you can take off the list or move to a "taking your time" list? The idea is for you to find something you can remove from the making-time-for list so you can add becoming more in touch with your mind, will, and spirit to the list. This is not an overnight change. Is it positively challenging? Yes. Is it overwhelmingly frightening? No. For example, deciding to find a scripture that resonates with you and reading that scripture every day for a week. On the first day, you read the scripture. On the second day, you read the scripture and write down why you chose it. On the third day, you read the scripture and write down in your own words what the scripture means to you. On the fourth and fifth days, you look up the scripture in different versions of the Bible and read them for further clarity. Make a note of any versions that positively stood out to you (examples: the language was easy to understand, or you gained a deeper meaning, or it directly reminded you of something you experienced). On the sixth day, you read the scripture from the original Bible and from one of the versions that stood out. Write down any additional clarity you received. On the seventh day, you read the scripture again and, in prayer, thank God for giving you this scripture. Next week, begin the process again with a new scripture. At the end of the month, you will have connected to four scriptures that have fed your mind, will, and spirit. Within one year, you will have spiritual connections with 48 scriptures. Wow!

Seasons come and go. When you make time, you prepare yourself to be ready for the right season when it comes. In contrast, when you don't make time, you risk not being ready and miss out on the right season when it comes your way. When you make time, you are demonstrating your spirit's renewal. The time is right and the season is right. The only thing missing is your decision to do this for yourself.

## Welcoming a season of rain, when the Spirit reigns at a higher level in your life.

Spiritual growth looks good on you. Aligning your mind, will, and spirit to God's will shows inside and out. It looks like springtime when the smallest bud appears on a plant. As you make time and continue to work through the process, the bud shows some of its colors. You smile more. Things that once upset you do not bother you anymore. Much like the fertilization process, your mind, will, and spirit are being fed the nutrients they need (found in a relationship with God) through the connection you have with scriptures that speak to you personally. And, as you continue to grow, you blossom. Much like the bud that emerges as a beautiful flower, full of color and fragrance, you emerge, refreshed and ready to spring into your purpose. As the refreshing showers of spring rain down on you, you become noticed, just like the flower that was once a small bud. Whatever your purpose is will be revealed to you in this season of blossoming, of emergence, of fulfillment.

## The power of doing your part. (Yes, you have a part to play in arriving.)

Your part is to read one scripture a week. It's as easy as this—follow what the spirit tells you, and do the right thing. It's as difficult as this—follow what the spirit tells you, and do the right thing. If necessary, read again what is in Chapter 3 about taking the limits off your trust, about God's message for you, and distractions. As the saying goes, "The struggle is real." This is not a new struggle. There was a man in the Bible named Paul. Paul's past was a colorful one before he chose to believe and have his spirit renewed. Paul wrote in the book of Romans, in chapter 7, verse 19, about how he struggled to do right. His exact words (according to the New Living Translation version of the Bible) were: "*I want to do what is good, but I don't. I don't want to do what is wrong, but I do it anyway.*" This is not meant to condone wrong behavior, but rather, to help you not feel like a failure if you also struggle in this area. This same Paul wrote 13 of the 27 books in The New Testament. These books are alive today and changing lives all over the world. That, my friends, does not sound like a failure.

# CHAPTER 5

# TIMES OF LIFE
# WHEN WE NEED SALT:
## *The Comfort Of A Pinch*

**H**aving comfort in your life, every day.

Life is filled with ups and downs. One minute everything is going so well that you have to pinch yourself
to go from disbelief to acceptance. Then something
happens that turns everything upside down. Finding
comfort leads us out of those moments. We can often
find comfort in the small things. Things like watching a

## TIMES OF LIFE WHEN WE NEED SALT:

baby discover its toes or like holding a bouquet of fragrant fresh flowers, or hearing waves soothingly lap on the shore, or even receiving that special loving pinch on the cheek from Grandma—not enough to hurt, just enough to make you feel loved. If these comfort moments played all day in our lives, life would be a breeze. But they don't.

There are countless songs about the joy and pain in life, and people go to any number of places or things to get comfort when pain happens. Some people find supportive comfort in a listening ear or a few kind words from friends, family, or even random strangers. Others may find it in a support group that meets regularly. Then there's the temporary comfort. Some find temporary comfort in food or binge-watching TV. Then there's false comfort. This is a form of temporary comfort that comes from consuming alcohol or drugs. False comfort complicates matters even more. Then there's real comfort. Real comfort is always available to you. You don't have to schedule an appointment. You don't have to worry about your most personal information being broadcast to others.

There is no residual harm or side effects. God's love provides us with real comfort any time, any place. Receiving real comfort is one of life's great blessings. Receiving the real comfort of a special loving pinch from a single scripture is a blessing that reassures us trouble does not last forever and guides us with the love of God.

## Comfort Without Complication.

The sad truth is this, temporary comfort and false comfort tend to carry consequences. Some consequences are mild, some are severe. Rather than criticize the effects of being sedentary in front of the TV, or the results of overeating, alcohol, or drug abuse, we desire this book in the *Just A Pinch* series to have an uplifting effect. We want to share with you the life benefits that are available when God's word in the scriptures becomes a part of your life. It is God's desire for you to have this comfort. You can see it for yourself. And you can have it. It all comes together when you allow yourself to trust God so you can Just Say The Word over yourself, your life, and your circumstances—when you make His way your way.

# TIMES OF LIFE WHEN WE NEED SALT:

### ❤ Love Speaks ❤
#### *About Finding Your Own Pinch of Comfort*

https://JustSayTheWord.Love/PinchOfComfort

## You Never Have to Leave Home Without It—Comfort at Your Fingertips.

If you scanned the QR CODE or typed the URL into your browser and then watched the short video clip, you saw how I used my cellphone to find a scripture. I pray you begin to use this easy technology for yourself. We can meet the Bible right where we are. Today, you can even let the Bible come to you, one wonderful pinch at a time! Wherever you go, your Bible will be right there with you. Think of it as comfort at your fingertips.

# CHAPTER 6

# SALT FOR A SWEET LIFE:

## *It's A Treasure Trove Of Secrets For Enhancing Life Today*

**T**he contents of your sweet life might be different from mine, and that's okay.

Perhaps you've heard the saying "experience is a good teacher." Because we all have different experiences in life, the lessons we learn are tailored to our specific needs. This happens as we read specific scriptures in the Bible. You and I can read the same scripture and receive a message from it that is relevant to our life at that moment. God's will for our life at that moment speaks to us through that scripture. It is one of the most wonderful and timeless treasures of scripture.

**You might wonder, "When does 'just a pinch of salt' make life sweet?" It happens every day.**
When I was a child, I loved eating watermelon with my older sister Connie. She introduced me to putting a pinch of salt on the watermelon when it wasn't naturally sweet. I remember how the salt improved the taste and made it sweet. Afterward, she and I would get straws and drink the salty-sweet juice at the bottom of the watermelon. These memories made me think about times in my life that were not very sweet—times when I went through sadness, struggles, and disappointments. Sometimes I could reach out to a friend, but friends were not always available. The one thing I could always count on to be there and to come through for me was that "just a pinch" of a favorite and specific scripture that gave me the hope and reassurance I needed. To this day, I rely upon that comfort from a pinch of scripture to make my life sweet.

**And a pinch will do—no need for a big quantity.**
In cooking, the term "season to taste" is often used instead of an exact measurement. In other words, add a pinch of seasoning and then taste the food to find out if you need more seasoning. If you need more, add another pinch and repeat the process. If you have ever tasted food with too much salt or too much pepper, then you can appreciate how following this process will give you the right ratio of seasoning to the food's natural flavors. Scriptures also can flavor your life a pinch at a time. When you start by focusing on one scripture a week, that pinch will add just the right amount of flavor to your life.

**Add a pinch at a time and taste the sweet effect on your life.**
There are significant differences between sprinters and distance runners. Sprinters run short, quick races that are usually over in less than two minutes. Distance runners follow a creed of "a steady pace wins the race." They cover distances of more than 26 miles that take hours to complete. Both types of runners are well-conditioned athletes. Sprinters do not run distances, and

distance runners do not run sprints. Another difference is that sprinters are confined to a stadium or a running track. Along the course of a distance run, the runner can enjoy the outdoors and be one with nature one methodical step at a time. The distance runner can see cityscapes and nature up close and personal— green fields, a bee on a flower, fields of flowers, lakes, detailed and ornate architecture, manicured lawns of modest homes, or sprawling mansions. They listen to early-morning birds singing to each other. They feel the cool air on their face. They smell early-morning coffee and baked goods being prepared, and the scent of grass wet with morning dew. Why is this significant here? It is significant because sweetening your life one pinch of scripture at a time is a distance run, not a sprint. As you begin the process explained in Chapter 4 of reading one scripture a week, the methodical steps you take each day will provide you with opportunities to see and understand the love that God has for you. As your understanding grows, so will your ability to trust God and hear from Him. As you trust God and hear from Him, your life will be sweetened. As your life is sweetened, you taste each flavorful bite, and you get the sweet effect a scripture has on your life like a distance runner savoring all of the beauty taken in during a peaceful run.

## Imagine a Water Bottle That's Always Full.

A water bottle is a very important piece of gear for someone going on a long hike. Keeping the body hydrated is extremely important. One of the measures used in hospitals to treat patients is to administer fluids to hydrate their bodies. So, the water bottle on the hike is survival equipment, just like the food and extra clothing in the backpack. On the hike, becoming dehydrated is unwise and can actually increase your susceptibility to unclear thinking and physical problems. A hiker's self-discipline to drink water at regular intervals is a survival skill.

Imagine a water bottle that's always full. Every time you need it, it is full. When you're thirsty, it refreshes you. When you lack self-discipline and become dehydrated, this water bottle is available, filled with the life-sustaining water that you need to restore yourself and get you back on track. Such a "water bottle" exists.

Such a source of restoration is real. It is always full and always available. In the course of reading this book, you have become acquainted with it. The refreshments I speak of are the scriptures in your Bible. As you have heard about them, I pray that you have also read them for yourself. As we hike through life, so many specific scriptures from The Bible help our lives to thrive and stay on track—like a water bottle that's always full.

## Imagine Your Bible as a Treasure Trove of Secrets That Enhances Your Life.

People enjoy finding treasure—a successful metal detector hunt on the beach that reveals a rare coin; the exciting moment acknowledging a winning lottery ticket; your laughing-and-crying-until-you-are-breathless celebration when you discover that you have *all* the winning PowerBall numbers. That winning feeling is euphoric. However, on the other side of the coin (pun intended) is that losing feeling. The money invested in those PowerBall lottery tickets—with a return of zero. Those hours spent combing the sand, beaten down by the sun, only to find nothing. Often in the gambles we take in life, the odds are not in our favor. If you prefer odds that are *always in your favor*, you will find them in your Bible. Assembled within its pages are nuggets of wisdom to guide you through your choices and your life. It is a treasure trove of scripture after scripture that will enhance your life by reassuring you of great and precious promises. Promises that tell you you are good enough. You are strong enough. Yes, you are beautiful. Yes, you are capable. Trouble does not last forever. This too shall pass. The pain will end. You are okay. You are loved. This treasure is as close as your printed Bible sitting across the room, and today right at hand in your cellphone, tablet, and computer. Now, imagine a simple routine for yourself of reading scripture a pinch at a time and strengthening your life.

**CHAPTER 7**

# HOW DO YOU KNOW
# WHICH WAY TO GO?

*Easy Navigation To The Secrets*

**H**ow do *you* know which way to go?

Speaking of that cellphone, technology has made it possible for you to drive from point A to point B using your cellphone's navigation system, even when you are not sure of which way to go. Perhaps you are feeling like you don't know which way to go when it comes to reading scriptures. After all, the Bible seems to have at least one ba-zillion pages—where do you even start?

Here is where I tell you a riddle. Question: How do you eat an elephant? Answer: One bite at a time. Similarly, a simple navigation system that leads you to the best of the Bible for you one bite at a time, "one pinch at a time" at any moment, takes away that feeling of not knowing where to start.

Waiting for you within those "ba-zillion" pages are individual scriptures that have wonderfully relevant answers to your questions. Scriptures that will uplift you, even when you're down. Scriptures that will dry your tears, soothe your worries, calm your fears, and direct your path.

**Navigating Life.**

As wonderful as a satellite navigation system is, I become quite frustrated when I'm directed to take turns that I know are guiding me away from my destination. I wonder why it is directing me to go west when my destination is east. It's even more irritating when I'm in a rush and have to arrive by a certain time. Sometimes I veer off the given course and go my own way. When I do this, the navigation system begins to spin and "redirect" to accommodate my new route. As long as I have the system activated, it is with me, providing directions to guide me to where I need to go.

I believe this characteristic of the navigation system took a page directly out of God's playbook. Being there for us is exactly how God operates. God has a plan and purpose for you, for me, and all of us. Throughout our life, He navigates a path for us to follow. Sometimes to us, the path doesn't make sense, but He knows what is best for us. When we veer off and do our own thing our way, He is still there. When we decide to activate, He is ready to get us back on the best path for us. Those detours and additional turns the navigation system recommends could be there to protect us from a road hazard that we are not aware of. Sometimes it's a matter of convenience. Turning right instead of left will put me at the front door, instead of on the other side of a busy road.

God places extra turns and detours in our life too—for our benefit. Some are there to protect us from hurt, harm, and danger. Some are there to allow us to experience something that our life needs. It could be an opportunity to become stronger, more patient, more accepting, or more obedient. A pinch of scripture found in the first book of Samuel, chapter 15, verse 22, says, "... *obedience is better than sacrifice*..." When we follow God's plan—even if it means sacrificing something *we think* is better—we come out ahead. Every inconvenience has another side. Once we reach our destination and settle in, we forget the inconvenience that we had labeled "the worst experience ever!"

## Lost and Found

Picture in your mind a parent walking with their young child on a busy street or in a crowded store. While the parent is holding the child's hand, the parent is providing love and guidance, safely taking the child where they need to go. The child is surrounded by all of this as long as the child is holding the parent's hand. The parent can provide it, because they are connected with the child, hand-in-hand. Now picture that for whatever reason, their hands come apart. Now the two are separated, and despite the countless warnings to not wander off, the child has moved away and is now lost. Unimaginable terror grips both of them while they are separated. Does the parent throw in the towel, say, "Oh, well," and go home? No! The parent does all they can to find their beloved child. They call out the child's name and very likely reach out for help from others to assist in the search. Any initial anger the parent possibly felt because the child ignored repeatedly being told to not wander off has been replaced by a flood of joy when the child is once again holding the parent's hand. The child's tear-drenched face, racing heart, and rapid breathing are calmed by the reunion hug given when the child runs to the parent's waiting arms.

The love between the parent and child and the child and parent is strong. The love God has for His children, for me and you, is stronger. When your hand is in God's hand and you open your heart to trust God, God provides protection, endless and unconditional love, and guidance—that navigation that you need in life. Those times in life when we separate from God, He is longing for us to reconnect with Him.

Just like that parent longing for the child to reconnect, God does not go someplace where you cannot find Him. He is speaking to you. He is calling out for you. Perhaps in your heart, you have felt it. Perhaps in the pages of this book, you received confirmation of an unfulfilled need. A longing for something you haven't been able to put your finger on. Consider this, it's not just your finger that is required. It is your whole heart. It's a surrender that does not take you down but rather lifts you up. Just like when the child reconnects with the parent, when you connect or reconnect with God, He does not respond with anger. He doesn't scold or say you had it coming. No—He lovingly accepts you just as you are. You do not have to fix yourself up, dust yourself off. Just trust Him, open your heart and give Him your hand. With your hand in His, you are in a position to receive what you need.

If you are looking for navigation, here is a pinch of scripture to give you some comfort. It is found in the book of Isaiah, chapter 41, verse 13, and it says,

"*For I the Lord your God, will hold your right hand, saying to you, Fear not, I will help you.*" God wants you to not be afraid. He wants to help you. He wants to hold your hand. He wants you to connect or reconnect with Him.

### *Say The Word—Action Step 2:*

Let's revisit the text messages from God in Chapter 3. As you recall, you were asked to thoughtfully respond to one of three text messages sent from God to you. Take a moment to revisit the text message you selected and the response you wrote. Now that you've read Chapters 4, 5, and 6, consider this:

- What would you change about the response you wrote to the message you chose in Chapter 3?
- How you would respond to the other two texts?
- Take a moment and write your responses to God for all three text messages. We have provided space for your responses below each text.

**Three (3) Text Messages From God to You:**
(from Chapter 3)

**God's Text #1:** "My child, what is stopping you from trusting me?"

**God's Text #2:** "My strong and limitless child, how easy or difficult is it when you attempt to go at life on your own?"

**God's Text #3:** "My beloved child, you need to get something off your chest. What do you need to tell me?"

Action Step 2 allows you to experience three different conversations that can take place between God and you. It shows the loving and gentle way that God relates to you, and it allows you to discover how you can communicate with God. You're on your way, and it can only get better from here.

**The satisfaction of words that reveal the way to go!**

God loves you so much that He provided a book full of scriptures to bring light to your life, a pinch at a time. In addition to the scriptures showing how much God loves you, scriptures also reveal the way to go—positive ways that put our lives on the right paths. If you feel like you've followed the map before and got lost, then perhaps it's because God has something better for you. The book of Psalms says in chapter 119, verse 105, *"Your word is a lamp for my feet, and a light for my path."* God loves you, and He has provided scriptures to remind you of this. His love is with you wherever you are.

### *Say The Word*—Action Step 3:

The choice is yours to do your part and become intentional about making time regularly, eventually daily, to seek God's word. You possess the tools to do this. Revisit chapter 4 and see **When you make time, it IS the right season**. Begin to act upon the list you made, and make daily scripture reading a part of your life.

### *Easy Navigation to the Best in the Bible for Your Life TODAY!*

My sincere hope and prayer, is that you choose to stay connected. To assist you in doing this, I invite you to take one simple step right now, and say, "YES!" to receive our weekly personal text message, *"JUST A PINCH: Scriptures for Living."* In this once-a-week message, we share a scripture and some words that apply the scripture to everyday life. It provides you with *Easy Navigation to the Best in the Bible for Your Life TODAY!* Simply scan the QR code below, or type the URL in a browser, and you will be directed to a page where you can take your first step right now to receive *"JUST A PINCH: Scriptures for Living."*

### 💙 Receive *"JUST A PINCH: Scriptures for Living"* 💙

https://JustSayTheWord.Love/GetJustAPinch

Printed in the USA
CPSIA information can be obtained
at www.ICGtesting.com
LVHW071950170923
758232LV00084B/815

9 781734 752878